MANAGE MY EMOTIONS

Kenneth Martz, Psy.D. & Meredith Martz

No part of this book may be reproduced in any form or by any means without the prior written permission of the publisher, except for brief quotes used in connection with reviews, written specifically for inclusion in a magazine or newspaper.

Warning – Disclaimer: The purpose of this book is to educate. This book is not intended to take the place of professional counseling. It is a tool to support anyone in their personal journey of growth. Consult your physician prior to beginning any physical exercise.

The author and/or publisher do not guarantee that anyone following these techniques, suggestions, tips, ideas or strategies will become successful. The author and/or publisher shall have neither liability nor responsibility to anyone with respect to any loss or damage caused, or alleged to be caused, directly or indirectly, by the information contained in this book.

1st Printing Edition, 2021

ISBN: 978-1-7357109-8-3 (print)

ISBN: 978-1-7357109-6-9 (digital)

www.DrKenMartz.com

Copyright © 2021 by Kenneth Martz

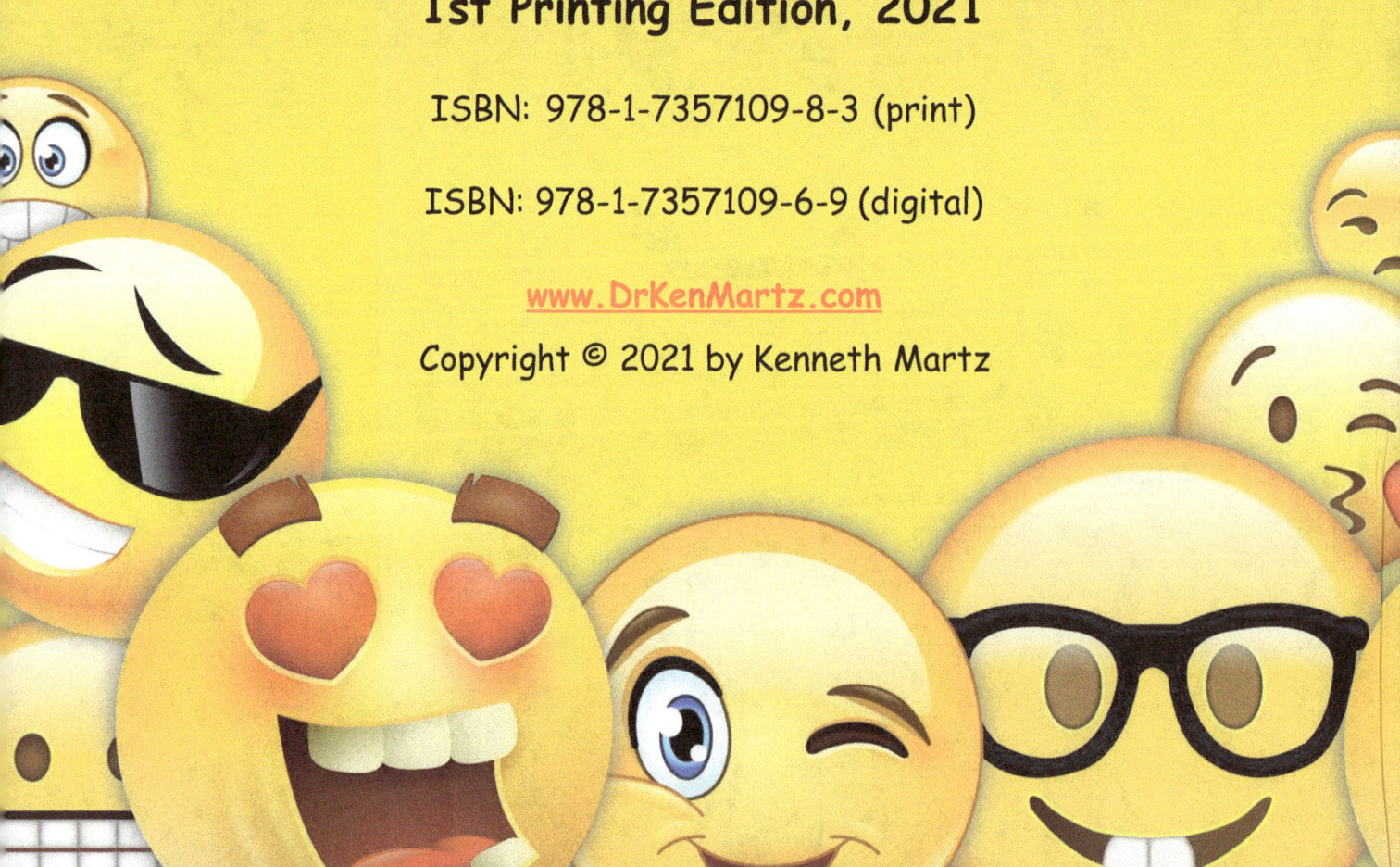

To The Hope And Promise Of Our Next Generation

Where Am I Now?

We all have a lot of different feelings. These can change quickly. Sometimes I am happy and at other times, I may be sad, mad, or scared.
Sometimes I can feel a bunch of feelings at once which can be confusing.

The Role of Emotions

Feelings can help me.
When I am scared, it warns me of danger.
When I am mad, it lets me know I want something important.

When I feel upset there are
lots of things I can do.

Talk to someone close to me
Take three deep slow breaths
Play a game
Talk to a friend
Color or paint
Play outside
Do jumping jacks

What are two other things I like to do?

Coping Skills

Feelings and Emotions

When I am feeling mad or sad,
what is it like for me?

Where do I feel it in my body?
Is it in my head, face, or maybe
my chest or belly?

What does it feel like?
Is it heavy, light or maybe
even tight?

What do I do?
Do I make a fist or frown?

Emotions and Learning

When I practice anything, I will get better.

When I practice, I will learn it more.
How can I practice being happy?

Tell a joke
Smile at someone
Play a game
Hug someone you love
Go on a playdate with a friend
Tell someone you trust two thing things you are thankful for

What are two other things I like to do?

The Six Big Emotions

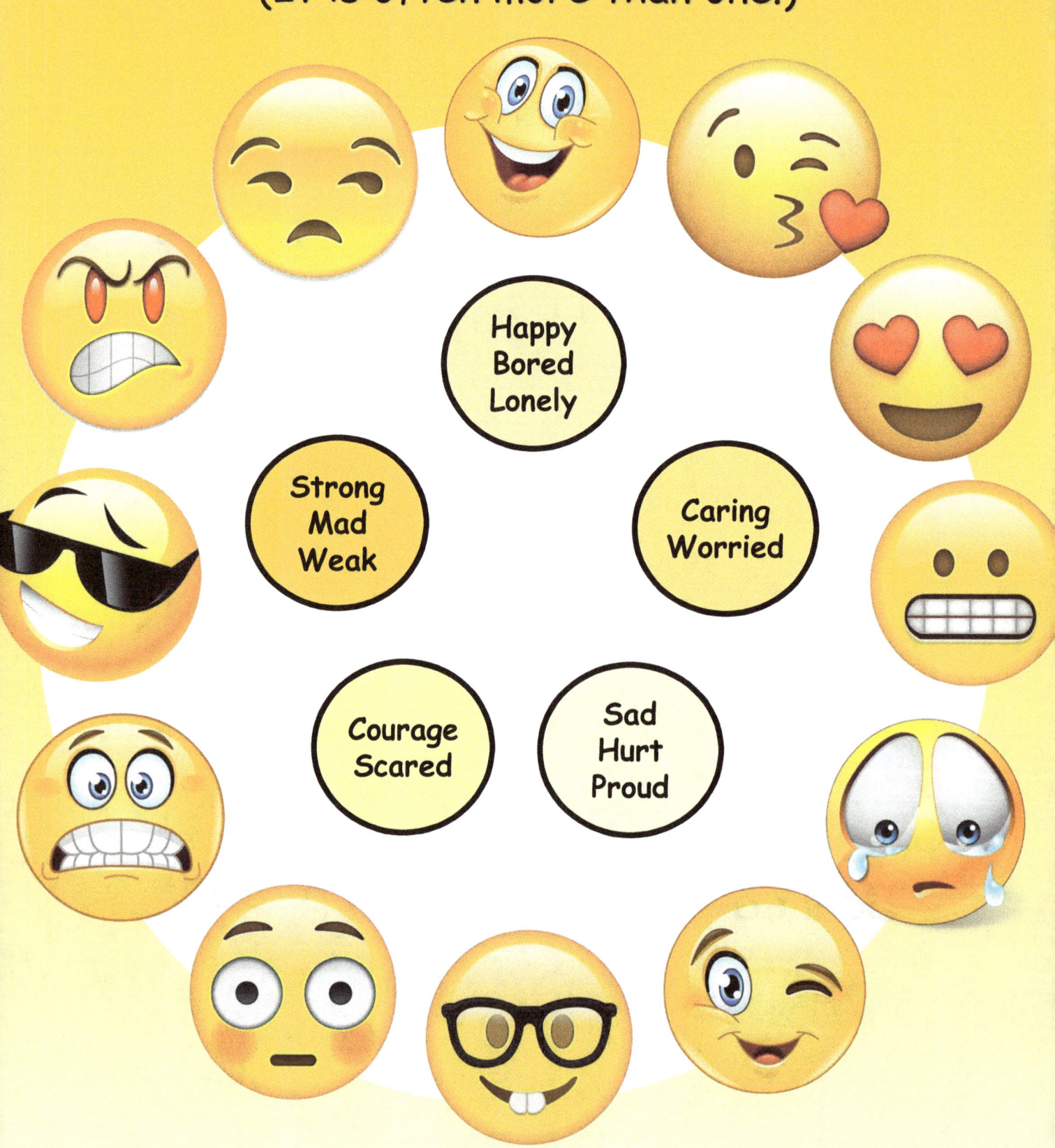

Practice

When I practice, I get better and stronger.

I can practice things to make me happy and proud by:

Making a list of important things
Repeating those things often.

Courage and Fear

Do Superman or Wonder Woman get scared?
Courage is doing something even though we are scared.

I can practice by:

Standing tall, lifting my chest and putting my hands on my hips, and feeling strong like my favorite hero.
Imagining a big hug from someone who knows I can do it.
Remembering, "I am strong."

What is one other thing that helps me feel strong?

Drive and Anger

Is it OK to be angry?

Yes. Anger means we know that we really want something important. ...And we still need to behave. No hitting or yelling.

When I am calmer, I can make better choices.

I can practice letting go of anger by:

Inhaling deeply. Then blow air out of my mouth very slowly, like blowing on hot food to cool it down. Every time I blow out air, I let the anger soften.

Doing some jumping jacks or physical activity for a few minutes.

What is one other thing that helps me feel calm?

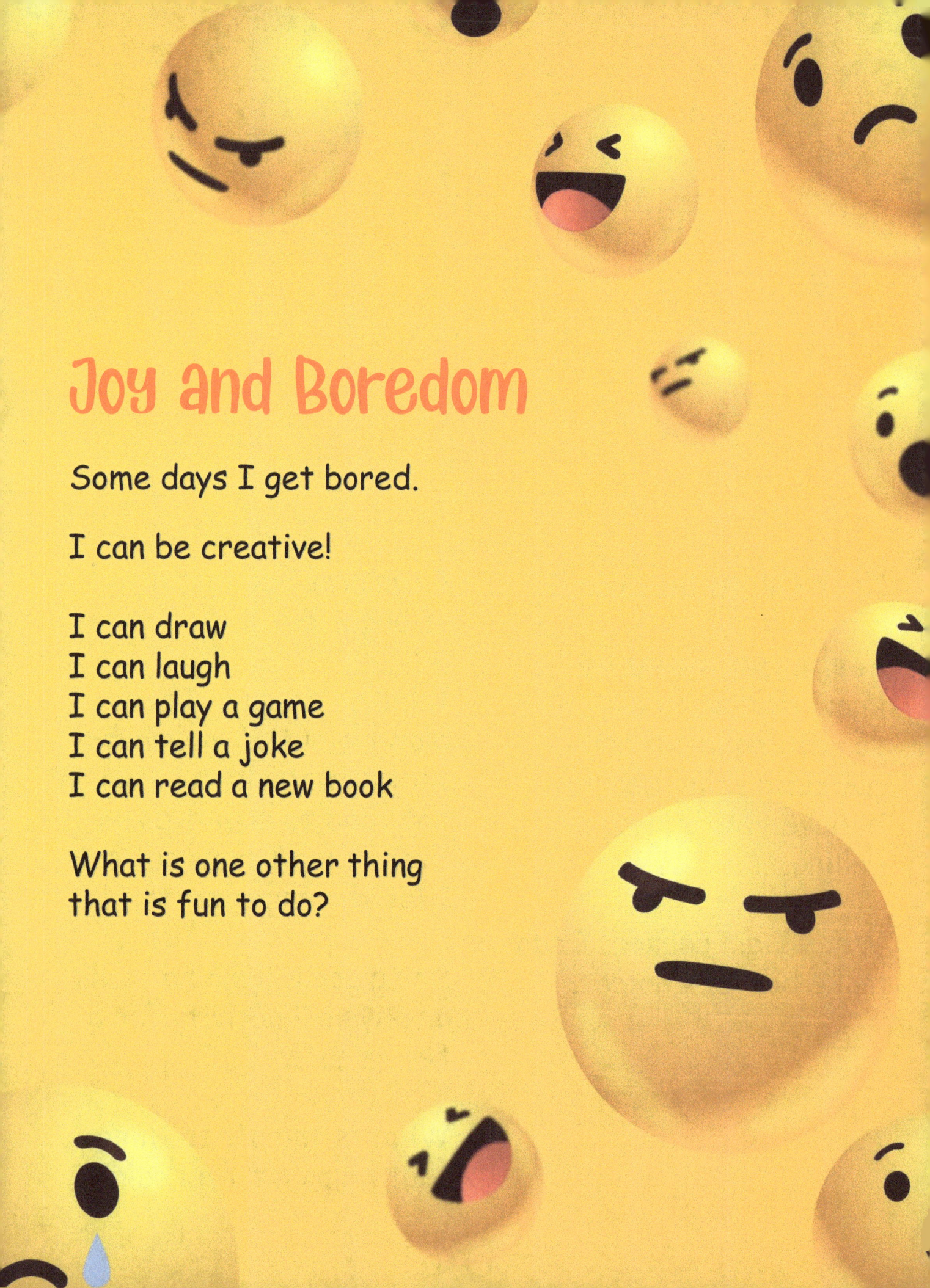

Joy and Boredom

Some days I get bored.

I can be creative!

I can draw
I can laugh
I can play a game
I can tell a joke
I can read a new book

What is one other thing that is fun to do?

Compassion and Worry

Some days I worry.

I can practice being confident by:

Imagine a big hug from a helpful adult
Feel the Earth supporting me from below
Inhale and exhale slowly, feeling each breath

Values and Sadness

When I value someone (or something), or love them a lot, I may feel sad or miss that person while they are away.

I can practice appreciation by:

Appreciating the things I have
Letting go of things I don't need
Cleaning my room
Writing a letter to the person I miss

Play the Thankful Game
- Take turns with a friend
- Each person says one thing they are thankful for
- Go as fast as you can
- Get as many as you can

Getting to Love

When I love someone, I may feel a lot of things.

I can practice helping the relationship:

- By helping clean up the dishes
- Playing games together
- Asking for help
- Giving warm hugs to the people I care about

Communication

Asking and Listening are Very Important
I can practice communication by:
Asking for things that I want
Knowing that sometimes I don't get what I ask for
Listening for what others want
Helping others when I can

Difficult Communication

Sometimes other kids say things that hurt.
Sometimes this is an accident.
Sometimes this is on purpose by a bully.
I can practice:
Keep my head up and shoulders back
Act brave and walk away without reacting
Remember I am strong
Talk to a helpful adult about it
Spend time with good friends

Relationships

I get different emotions when I am with different people, like friends, teachers, brothers and sisters.

How quickly can I practice the things I've learned?

School

At school, I may:
Get scared by a bully
Be worried about passing a test
Be happy to play with my friends

I can practice ahead of time:
Spending time with helpful friends
Studying just a little bit extra
Joining a club to spend time with friends

Culture

There are people that live
all around the world.
Some look like me, and
some don't.
Sometimes they have new
ideas or games.
There are lots of new ideas
to explore!

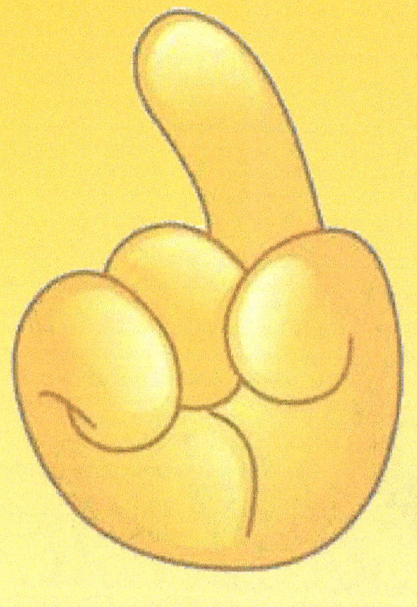

Next Steps

Remember and Repeat These Words Often

I am Strong

I am Friendly

I am Helpful

I am Worthy

I am Loved

I am Enough

My Mistakes Help Me Grow

The World Is a Safe Place

I Get Better Every Single Day

About the Authors

Dr. Ken Martz is a licensed psychologist with more than 25 years experience. He is the bestselling author of <u>Manage My Emotions: What I Wish I'd Learned in School about Anger, Fear, and Love</u>

Meredith Martz is a high school student. She is an avid reader. She is also a member of the National Charity League, donating her time in community service to children and older adults in need.

Visit us to learn more and receive free resources at www.DrKenMartz.com

For Parents and Guardians

As a parent and educator, I want to emphasize the importance of emotional balance as a part of healthy growth and development.

This book may be read by a child alone or together with the parents.

Please visit our website to obtain a copy of the <u>Manage My Emotions Parent's Guide.</u> This free resource offers tips on how to begin conversations about emotions with your child and help to get the most out of this book.
You can access the download page directly through the link below.

https://drkenmartz.com/mmek-request

www.ingramcontent.com/pod-product-compliance
Lightning Source LLC
Chambersburg PA
CBHW082042200426
43209CB00053B/1530